DISCARD

Mt. Juliet-Wilson County Library
2765 N. Mt. Juliet Rd.
Mt. Juliet, TN 37122
615-758-7051

HOW DO THEY MAKE THAT?

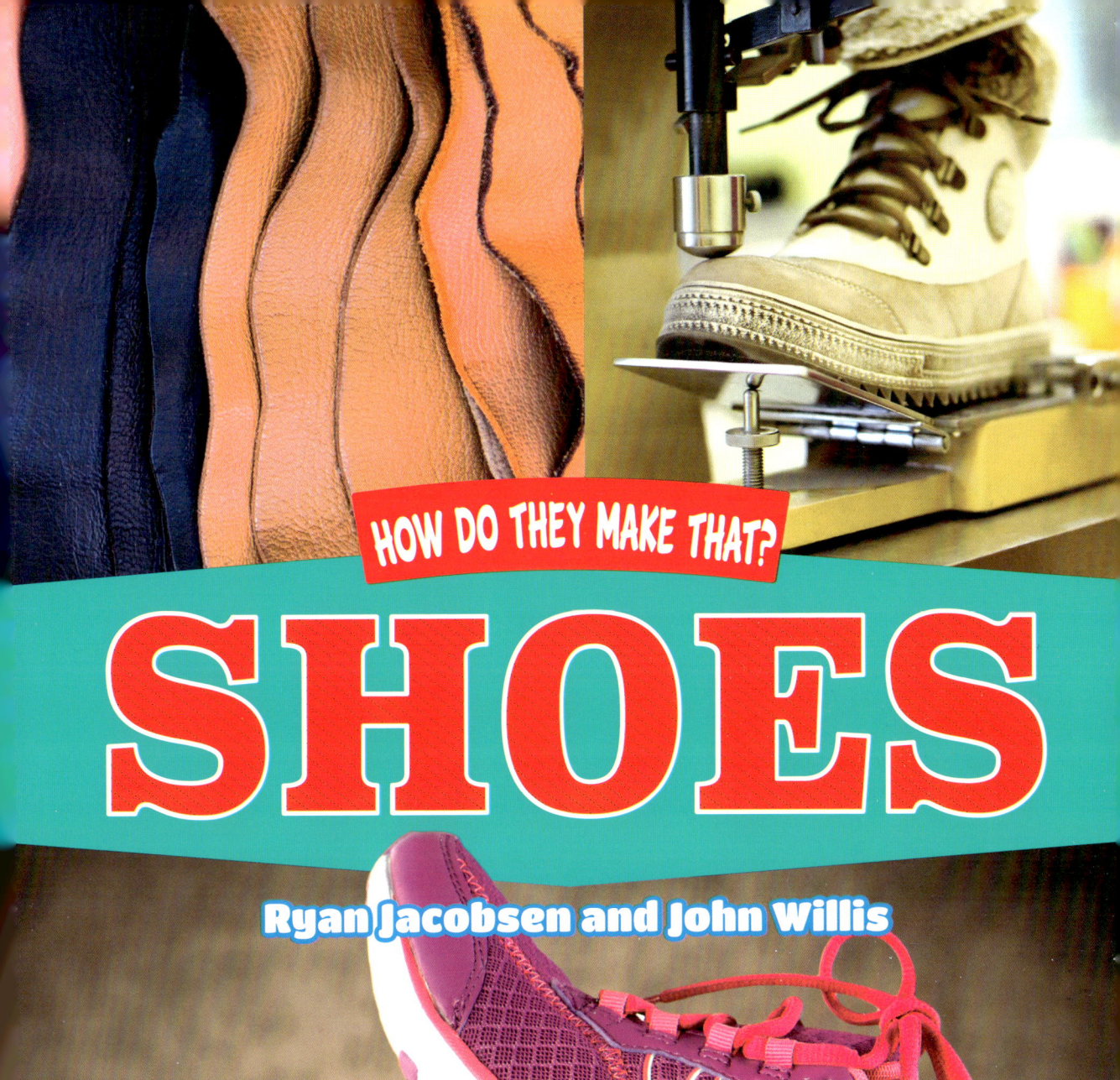

SHOES

Ryan Jacobsen and John Willis

www.av2books.com

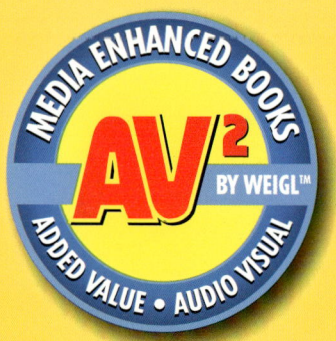

AV² provides enriched content that supplements and complements this book. Weigl's AV² books strive to create inspired learning and engage young minds in a total learning experience.

Your AV² Media Enhanced books come alive with...

Audio
Listen to sections of the book read aloud.

Key Words
Study vocabulary, and complete a matching word activity.

Video
Watch informative video clips.

Quizzes
Test your knowledge.

Embedded Weblinks
Gain additional information for research.

Slide Show
View images and captions, and prepare a presentation.

Try This!
Complete activities and hands-on experiments.

... and much, much more!

Go to www.av2books.com, and enter this book's unique code.

BOOK CODE

U766629

AV² by Weigl brings you media enhanced books that support active learning.

Published by AV² by Weigl
350 5th Avenue, 59th Floor
New York, NY 10118
Website: www.av2books.com

Copyright © 2017 AV² by Weigl
All rights reserved. No part of this publication may be reproduced, stored in a retrieval system, or transmitted in any form or by any means, electronic, mechanical, photocopying, recording, or otherwise, without the prior written permission of the publisher.

Library of Congress Cataloging-in-Publication Data

Names: Jacobsen, Ryan, author | and Willis, John, author.
Title: Shoes / Ryan Jacobson.
Description: New York, NY : AV2 by Weigl, [2017] | Series: How do they make that? | Includes bibliographical references and index.
Identifiers: LCCN 2016005662 (print) | LCCN 2016006699 (ebook) | ISBN 9781489645418 (hard cover : alk. paper) | ISBN 9781489650030 (soft cover : alk. paper) | ISBN 9781489645425 (Multi-user ebk.)
Subjects: LCSH: Shoes--Juvenile literature. | Shoe industry--Juvenile literature.
Classification: LCC TS990 .J33 2017 (print) | LCC TS990 (ebook) | DDC 338.4/7685/31--dc23
LC record available at http://lccn.loc.gov/2016005662

Printed in the United States of America in Brainerd, Minnesota
1 2 3 4 5 6 7 8 9 0   20 19 18 17 16

072016
210716

Project Coordinator: John Willis   Art Director: Terry Paulhus

Every reasonable effort has been made to trace ownership and to obtain permission to reprint copyright material. The publishers would be pleased to have any errors or omissions brought to their attention so that they may be corrected in subsequent printings.

Weigl acknowledges Getty Images and iStock as its primary image suppliers for this title.

Contents

AV² Book Code	2
We All Use Shoes	4
Making Leather	8
At the Shoe Factory	10
Getting into Shape	16
Good Looks	24
Onto Your Feet	28
Quiz	30
Key Words/Index	31
Log on to www.av2books.com	32

We All Use Shoes

We wear shoes every day. We have different shoes for different reasons. We play in our tennis shoes. We put on dress shoes for holidays. We bring sandals to the beach. We wear boots to play in the snow. Some people even rent shoes for weddings. We want our shoes to feel comfortable. They keep our feet safe from sharp things such as glass. They keep our toes warm. We want our shoes to look nice, too. Do you have a favorite pair of shoes? What kind are they? What do they look like?

Shoes come in many different shapes, colors, and sizes.

Shoe laces need to be long enough to tie into a knot.

All shoes have the same basic parts. The top is called the upper. It covers your foot and wraps around the sides. Your foot goes beneath the upper. It rests on the **insole**. There is also a **sole**. The sole is the very bottom of the shoe. It is the part of the shoe that leaves footprints. Many shoes have laces or strings to tie together. If they do, they also have a tongue. This is the flap at the top.

Have you thought about how shoes are made? There are many steps. Shoes are made from many things. Some shoes might have rubber, cloth, plastic, or even wood. Many shoes also use **leather**. This is made out of animal skin. The most common skin used is from a cow.

Making Leather

Cow skin is sent to a **tannery**. This is a factory where leather is made. Workers treat the skin with special **chemicals**. The chemicals make the hair fall off the skin. Then, workers put the skin in a kind of salt. This turns the skin into leather. Workers dye the leather brown. They also add more chemicals to the leather. This makes it stronger. Then, the leather is shipped to the shoe factory.

Cow skins are not the only skins that can become leather. Leather is also made from pigs, goats, sheep, alligators, snakes, and other animals.

Once leather is formed, it can be dyed into many different colors.

At the Shoe Factory

For many people, the way a shoe looks is just as important as how it fits. That is why shoes are designed by artists. They sketch ideas for how the shoes will look. Artists might draw dozens of different ideas before a design is chosen.

The final design it is sent to the clicking department. The design is drawn again. This time it is drawn on a **mold** shaped like a foot. It shows workers what the finished shoe will look like. People's feet are different sizes, so shoes need to be designed in different sizes, too. For this reason, the mold can be stretched apart and pushed together. It is used to design different sizes of shoes.

There can be up to 200 different steps when making a shoe.

Shoes 11

Workers first make the top of each shoe. This is the upper. A clicking operative does this step. This worker uses a pattern to cut leather by hand.

After the pieces are cut, workers send them through a splitting machine. This machine shaves off a layer from the leather. All of the pieces of the leather are now the same thickness. Next, workers use a skiving machine. It cuts the leather's edges. The leather becomes thin. The thin edges are easier to sew together.

Leather has a **natural pattern** to it. Pieces for the left and right shoe need to look the same. The clicking operative cuts leather so that the natural designs are the same but opposite one another. If a clicking operative makes a mistake, the left and right shoes will not match.

The clicking department's main job is to take the design of the shoe and create the upper.

Shoes 13

The leather next goes to the closing department. The pieces of the upper are ready to be put together. The first pieces are sewn on a flat machine. The upper becomes curved and does not lie flat. It starts to look like a shoe. Workers now switch to a post machine. They finish sewing the upper.

Another worker hammers the stitches to smooth and flatten them. Then, a worker glues leather strips around the upper's edges. The strips cover the upper's open sides. Last, the **eyelets** are added. These are the holes for shoelaces.

The closing department makes a flat piece of leather look like a real shoe.

Shoes 15

A person who made shoes used to be called a cobbler.

16   How Do They Make That?

Getting into Shape

Next, it is the lasting department's turn. Workers put a soft **lining** inside the uppers. Each upper goes around a plastic mold in the shape of a foot. It is called a **last**. The last keeps the upper in the shape of a shoe while the bottom is put together.

The bottom begins with an insole. The insole is glued to the upper's lining.

Grinding helps the bottom of the shoe absorb glue by giving it an even surface.

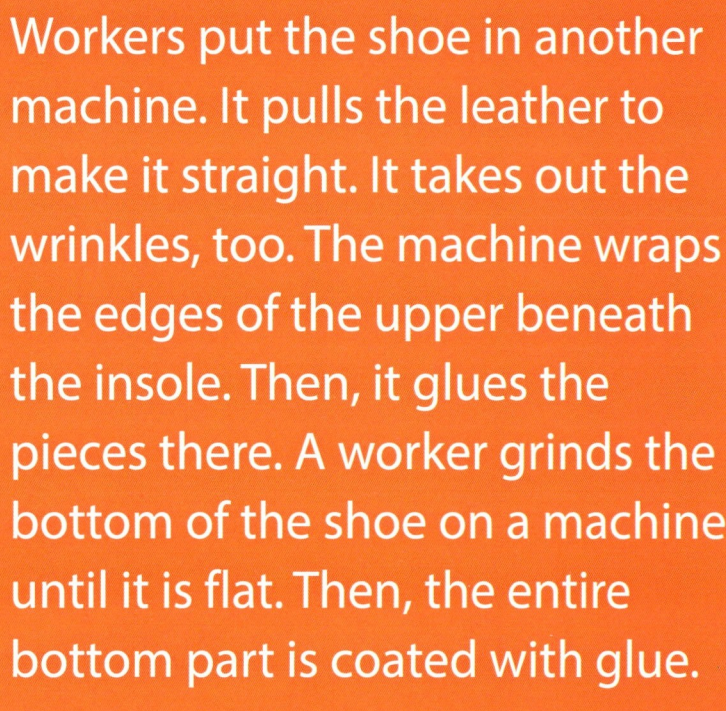

Workers put the shoe in another machine. It pulls the leather to make it straight. It takes out the wrinkles, too. The machine wraps the edges of the upper beneath the insole. Then, it glues the pieces there. A worker grinds the bottom of the shoe on a machine until it is flat. Then, the entire bottom part is coated with glue.

The shoe must be completely put together around the last. This makes the shoe have the right shape. After the shoe is finished, the last is stuck inside. To remove the last, workers take off the insole. They take out the last. Then, they glue the insole back into place.

Workers make the sole of the shoe from leather, plastic, rubber, or wood. They shape it with cutting tools or a mold. Workers pour hot liquid material into a mold. The mold is a hollow container that is the shape of the sole. When the liquid cools, it becomes hard. Then, it is taken out of the mold.

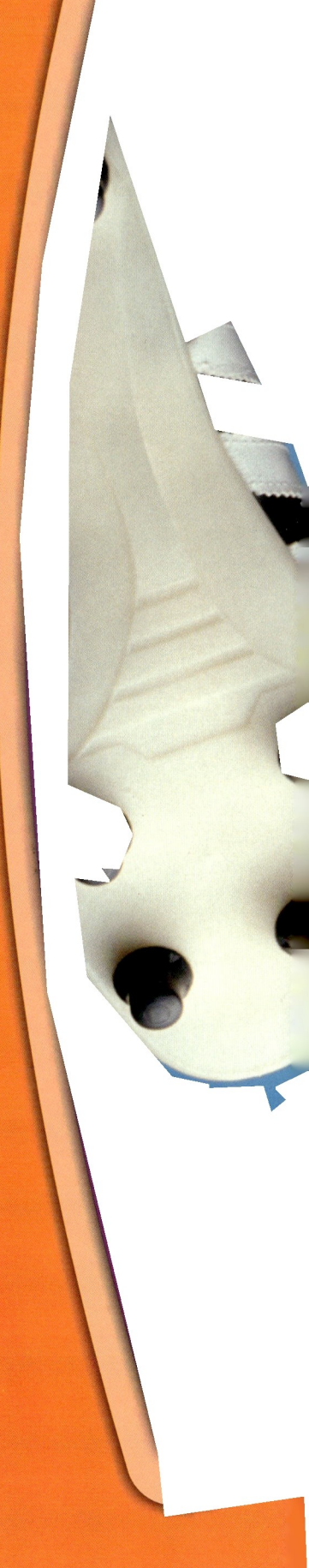

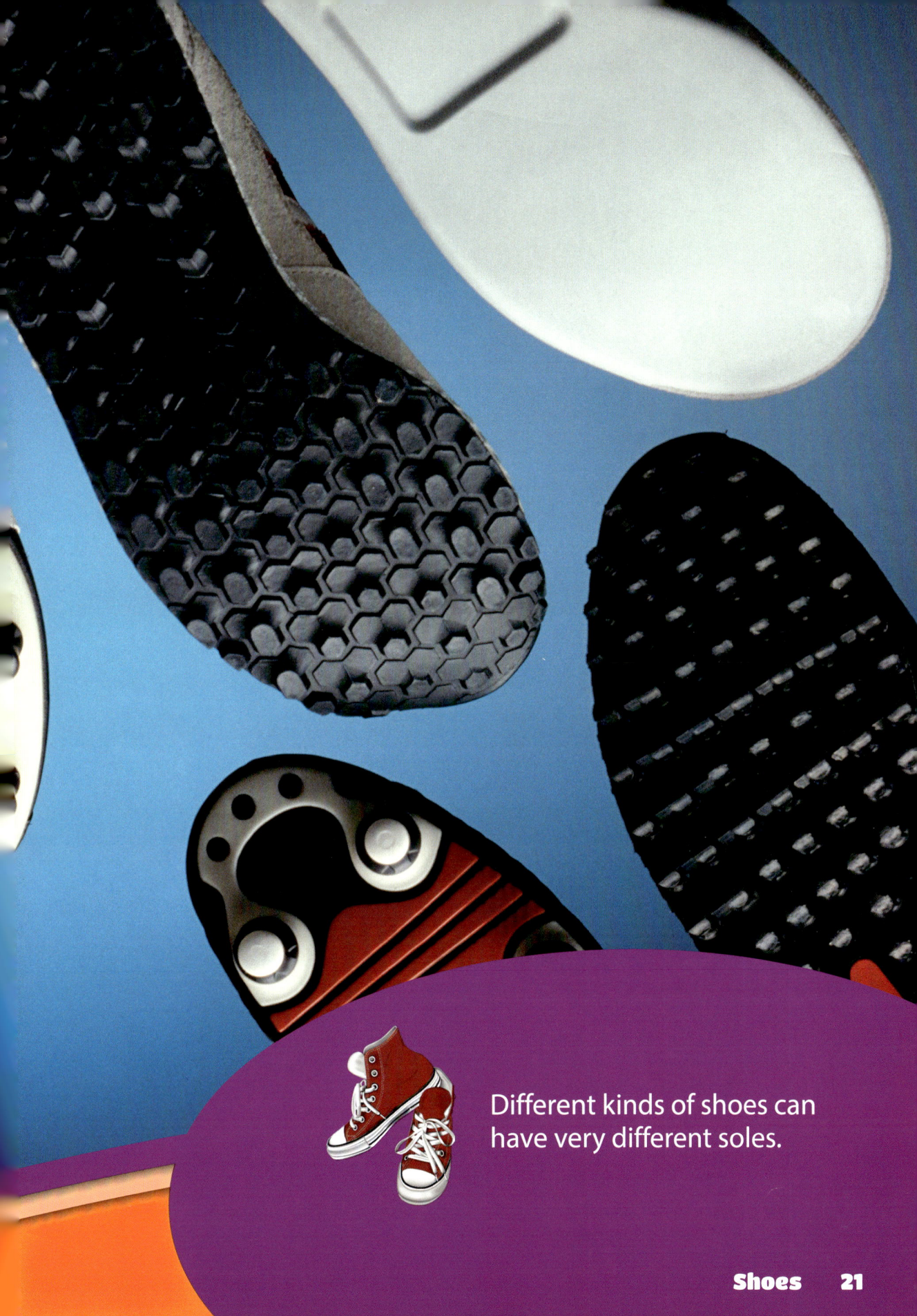

Different kinds of shoes can have very different soles.

Shoes 21

Workers press the sole onto the glue at the bottom of the shoe. After about ten minutes, the glue dries.

It holds the sole in place. When the upper and sole are glued together, it makes a complete shoe.

A shoe's glue must be very strong.to keep the sole attached while it is being worn.

Shoes 23

Heels are ground down to make sure they are even and comfortable.

24   How Do They Make That?

Good Looks

The shoes are not done yet. Their next stop is the finishing department. Workers trim the soles to make them smooth and even. They apply **stain** to color the shoes. They polish the shoes. This makes them look clean and new. The shoelaces are laced in the eyelets. Then, workers glue tags and labels inside the shoes.

The finished shoes are tested. Some tests are done by people. Other tests are done by machines. The tests make sure the shoes have been made the right way.

A box helps keep pairs of shoes together when they are shipped all over the world.

26 How Do They Make That?

Next, each pair of shoes is put into a box. They are bundled with other boxes and wrapped in plastic for shipping.

Now they can be loaded onto trucks and shipped to shoe stores.

The average adult woman owns 17 pairs of shoes.

Onto Your Feet

Shoes arrive at sports stores, department stores, and shoe stores. Some stores put all the boxes out. They set them together by style and size. Other stores put out just one pair. Then, a store worker finds your size and helps you try on the shoes. People can also buy shoes on the internet. They find their size and the style they like. Then, the shoes are sent right to their homes.

What kind of shoes do you like best? Are blue flats or red sneakers your style? You can pick shoes with stripes or checker designs on them, too. Be sure to try them on, though. You want them to feel just right. They should not be too tight or too loose. Did you find the right fit? Good. Enjoy your new shoes.

A child's foot grows every year.

Shoes 29

Quiz

Match the steps with the pictures.

- A. Tannery
- B. Shoe design
- C. Clicking department
- D. Closing department
- E. Lasting department
- F. Finishing department

Answers: 1.B 2.C 3.A 4.F 5.E 6.D

Key Words

chemicals: substances made using chemistry

eyelets: small round holes in leather that are used to thread laces through

insole: the part inside a shoe that your foot rests upon

last: a piece of hard plastic that is shaped like a foot

leather: chemically treated animal skin that can be used for clothing or furniture

lining: a material that covers the inside of something

mold: a hollow container that you put something into to set its shape or a solid piece used to hold the shape of something

sole: the bottom part of a shoe

stain: a dye that is used to color leather or wood

tannery: a place where animal skin is made into leather

Index

clicking department 10, 13, 30
clicking operative 12
closing department 14, 30
cow 7, 8

eyelets 14, 25

finishing department 25, 30

lasting department 17, 30
leather 7, 8, 9, 12, 14, 15, 19, 20

shoe design 10, 12, 13, 30
shoelaces 14, 25
skiving machine 12
stain 25

tannery 8, 30

Log on to www.av2books.com

AV² by Weigl brings you media enhanced books that support active learning. Go to www.av2books.com, and enter the special code found on page 2 of this book. You will gain access to enriched and enhanced content that supplements and complements this book. Content includes video, audio, weblinks, quizzes, a slide show, and activities.

AV² Online Navigation

Audio
Listen to sections of the book read aloud.

Book Pages
AV² pages directly correspond to pages in the book.

Video
Watch informative video clips.

Embedded Weblinks
Gain additional information for research.

Key Words
Study vocabulary, and complete a matching word activity.

Try This!
Complete activities and hands-on experiments.

Quizzes
Test your knowledge.

Slide Show
View images and captions, and prepare a presentation.

AV² was built to bridge the gap between print and digital. We encourage you to tell us what you like and what you want to see in the future.

Sign up to be an AV² Ambassador at www.av2books.com/ambassador.

Due to the dynamic nature of the Internet, some of the URLs and activities provided as part of AV² by Weigl may have changed or ceased to exist. AV² by Weigl accepts no responsibility for any such changes. All media enhanced books are regularly monitored to update addresses and sites in a timely manner. Contact AV² by Weigl at 1-866-649-3445 or av2books@weigl.com with any questions, comments, or feedback.